AN IDEAS INTO ACTION GUIDEBOOK

Do You Really Need a Team?

IDEAS INTO ACTION GUIDEBOOKS

Aimed at managers and executives who are concerned with their own and others' development, each guidebook in this series gives specific advice on how to complete a developmental task or solve a leadership problem.

LEAD CONTRIBUTORS	Michael E. Kossler
	Kim Kanaga
GUIDEBOOK ADVISORY GROUP	Victoria A. Guthrie
	Cynthia D. McCauley
	Russ S. Moxley
DIRECTOR OF PUBLICATIONS	Martin Wilcox
EDITOR	Peter Scisco
WRITER	Janet Fox
DESIGN AND LAYOUT	Joanne Ferguson
CONTRIBUTING ARTISTS	Laura J. Gibson
	Chris Wilson, 29 & Company

CCL No. 412
ISBN No. 1-882197-66-6

CENTER FOR CREATIVE LEADERSHIP
POST OFFICE BOX 26300
GREENSBORO, NORTH CAROLINA 27438-6300
336-288-7210

Do You Really Need a Team?

Michael E. Kossler and Kim Kanaga

**Center for
Creative Leadership**

leadership. learning. life.

THE IDEAS INTO ACTION GUIDEBOOK SERIES

This series of guidebooks draws on the practical knowledge that the Center for Creative Leadership (CCL) has generated in the course of more than thirty years of research and educational activity conducted in partnership with hundreds of thousands of managers and executives. Much of this knowledge is shared – in a way that is distinct from the typical university department, professional association, or consultancy. CCL is not simply a collection of individual experts, although the individual credentials of its staff are impressive; rather it is a community, with its members holding certain principles in common and working together to understand and generate practical responses to today's leadership and organizational challenges.

The purpose of the series is to provide managers with specific advice on how to complete a developmental task or solve a leadership challenge. In doing that the series carries out CCL's mission to advance the understanding, practice, and development of leadership for the benefit of society worldwide. We think you will find the Ideas Into Action Guidebooks an important addition to your leadership toolkit.

Other guidebooks currently available:

- *Ongoing Feedback: How to Get It, How to Use It*
- *Becoming a More Versatile Learner*
- *Reaching Your Development Goals*
- *Giving Feedback to Subordinates*
- *Three Keys to Development: Defining and Meeting Your Leadership Challenges*
- *Feedback That Works: How to Build and Deliver Your Message*
- *Communicating Across Cultures*
- *Learning from Life: Turning Life's Lessons into Leadership Experience*
- *Keeping Your Career on Track: Twenty Success Strategies*
- *Preparing for Development: Making the Most of Formal Leadership Programs*
- *Choosing an Executive Coach*
- *Setting Your Development Goals: Start with Your Values*

Table of Contents

EXECUTIVE BRIEF

Despite all of the attention and accolades that organizations place on teams, they are not always the most efficient way to meet a business challenge. It's expensive and time consuming to launch a team, and it's a full-time job to lead a team toward achieving organizational objectives. This guidebook was written to help managers determine if a team is the right tool for meeting a business goal, and explains potential obstacles and challenges to forming a team that can operate at its full potential.

Teams — Fast Track or Trendy Trap?

Many organizations take great pride in describing themselves as "team-based." Scores of business books and magazine articles glorify and exalt teamwork over just about every other kind of organizational initiative. It's easy to see why. Information technology and the competition of global markets have created flatter organizations, which have turned to teams to replace a top-down approach to addressing business challenges and to supplant individual effort with group strength. Teams have enabled some companies to take giant leaps forward in such areas as time to market, innovation, customer service, and quality of goods and services.

But teams are not always the best way to accomplish a job. In their enthusiasm for teams, especially "high performance" teams, organizations often ignore the difficulties and costs of forming and launching teams. Teams typically need more time and more training to achieve results than do other kinds of work units. Teams may run counter to a company's established culture and reward systems. These challenges can block a team from operating at peak performance.

When assigned to the right task, comprised of the right people, and supported in the right environment, teams can achieve breakthrough performance. Determining if those three measures are met is a critical first step that many managers pass by in their zeal to build a team that can benefit their organization. This guidebook will help you determine if a team is the right way to accomplish the job your organization has assigned to you.

7

How Teams Work

Teams are often temporary groups, yet they can help an organization build its long-term competitive strength by discovering new products and services, by developing new ways of serving customers and clients, and by creating new systems that enhance an organization's efficiency.

If your organization has charged you with an important business initiative, it's possible that you may need to form a team to address that challenge. But before you start recruiting, determine whether a team really is the best way to achieve results. For many kinds of work it's more efficient and less expensive to have individuals or workgroups handle the job.

Teams Are Good for Complex Tasks

Teams are often the best choice for addressing complex problems and issues that affect many parts of the organization. Examples might include enterprise resource planning and implementation, a strategy for expanding the organization's products and services into the global market, or the development of an Internet business model. Through its members, a team can represent the thinking of a broad spectrum of stakeholders and act accordingly.

Teams can also help address controversial organizational change. When an organization expects resistance to a resource realignment, for example, or to a new business initiative, teams can increase the speed at which new ideas are accepted and help spread commitment to new strategies by communicating through its members to the company's different functional areas.

8

When Company X acquired Company Y, the leaders of the newly combined entity formed integration teams using members from both companies. The teams cut down on the "them versus us" mentality, chose the best elements from each organization's processes and culture to create new business systems, and diverted employee energy away from complaining and sabotage toward constructive problem solving and cooperation.

Simple, straightforward tasks don't demand a team. Teams seldom perform well right from the start (it takes time for people who don't know each other and who don't normally work together to merge their different interests and viewpoints into a team). Given that limitation, it would be difficult for you to justify the expense of setting up a team to accomplish a simple task with a short timeframe.

Company A wanted a fresh look for its printed materials, including a new logo and slogan. The decision to create an updated image was tied closely to the company's new vision statement and to its new global strategy. The company's management didn't create a team for the job but instead handed it to a few individuals in the corporate communications group, which worked with an outside design agency. The organization achieved participation and endorsement from other areas of the company using surveys and presentations that required few other resources.

Teams Are Good for Innovation

If your organization has assigned a challenge to you but isn't sure what the solution should be and hasn't been able to articulate an approach to solving the challenge, forming a team can be your best strategy. Teams are excellent vehicles for driving toward innovative, elegant, even unexpected answers to thorny business problems.

Teams spark innovation because they create a climate in which different opinions and viewpoints rub against one another. The friction among members can lead to creative perspectives that outpace what any individual might have otherwise achieved. Teams can produce results that can't be predicted from knowing the individual qualities and strengths of its members.

> *Organization B needed to cut 15 percent from its operating budget. Top management decided that it wouldn't simply lay off workers to reach the bottom line. Instead, it created a cross-functional team and gave it the goal of proposing ways to trim the budget without sacrificing quality or people.*

A team can be an effective engine for imagining and designing new systems, structures, and processes. But once the system is in place (or for any established system for that matter), managing the system doesn't require a team – in fact, it's an extravagant waste of time and energy to create a team to manage a familiar system.

> *In developing an organizational presence on the Internet, Company C formed an alliance with a technology company to develop a content-rich Web site that it hoped would drive new customers to its products and services. With little experience in content development, Company C formed a cross-functional team to create a system for finding, evaluating, and producing content from the knowledge it had gained over many years in the marketplace. After the system was in place and working to satisfaction, Company C turned over the development process to a workgroup so that the team members could return their attention to their original functions.*

The Way We Work

Look around your organization and you will find several types of work units. Broadly speaking, an organization can bring five categories of units (individual, workgroup, collaborative workgroup, team, and high-performance team) to bear on business challenges. By understanding how each of these work units gets results, you can determine which of them has the degree of collaboration you need to achieve the organization's goal. If your task doesn't require a great deal of interdependent collaboration, you don't need a team to meet your business objectives.

Team or Teamwork?

Some of the unquestioned enthusiasm organizations hold for teams has to do with the high value they place on teamwork. By equating teams with teamwork, some organizations create misperceptions about teams that become obstacles to the team's achieving results. Teamwork means cooperation. It calls for an awareness and respect for the contributions of others. It asks for a helpful and supportive attitude, as opposed to a hostile and adversarial one.

Teamwork is a valuable attribute in any joint endeavor, but such cooperation doesn't turn a group into a team. A team is a unit formed to achieve specific results – winning a game, managing an organization, or developing a new product. In other words, individuals working well together is ideal, but team members working together enhances results.

Individual

Some kinds of work can and should be handled by a single person. That individual has all the expertise, knowledge, and skills needed to do the job and is solely accountable for getting the job done. If the workload increases so that one person can no longer handle it, the company can create additional positions.

Workgroup

This work unit consists of a group of people who may work together and may all do essentially the same kind of work but who are not dependent on each other for information and skills needed to accomplish the job. For instance, the regional sales managers of a large national company would constitute a workgroup, even though they aren't located in the same office. In a human resources department of a large organization, all staff members with responsibilities for administering benefits could be considered a workgroup. They all perform similar or related tasks, but the amount of work is too large for one person.

Collaborative Workgroup

This is a common work unit category. Individuals in such a group need information from one another in order to achieve results. The work might be handed off from one individual to another, as in a manufacturing system. Each individual completes one step in a complex process that leads to a finished product. In collaborative workgroups, one person's errors in execution affect the ability of others in the group to do their work.

Well-functioning collaborative workgroups may look like teams, but they differ in that each individual is accountable for his or her work and is rewarded for individual performance. Another difference is that collaborative workgroups are most often permanent parts of an organization (a department, division, or branch office, for example), but teams are more often created to perform a specific task and dissolved when the mission has been completed.

Team

A team is a small group of interdependent individuals who collectively have the expertise, knowledge, and skills needed to

---

When Is a Team Not a Team?

Sports provides our most common model for what teams are and how they operate. But not all athletic units fit the description of teams. Wrestling teams, golf teams, and swim teams, for example, are groups of people all of whom perform the same or similar tasks. Each person in the group may train individually. During training and competition, the group members don't need to cooperate or even communicate with one another. They perform separately, one at a time. These kinds of teams are, using the definitions provided in this guidebook, more akin to workgroups.

Soccer, basketball, and baseball teams, on the other hand, bring together people with different and complementary skills. No individual player can win a game. All team members need to know what the game strategy is so that they can play their individual roles accordingly. What actions each player takes, and when, depends to some extent on what other members of the team do. The members of the team are interdependent. This interdependency and shared purpose is part of what we mean by *team*. Those same qualities are reflected in teams that work in the business world.

---

complete an assigned task or ongoing work. Team members have clear roles and responsibilities, share a vision and sense of purpose, and are collectively accountable for completing tasks and reaching the team's goal. It's harder to create a team than a workgroup or a collaborative workgroup. In organizational cultures that prize individual achievement, building and leading an effective team can be very difficult.

High-performance Team

A high-performance team exhibits an unusual degree of synergy among its members and exceeds performance expectations given its individual contributors. The personal commitment on the part of each member to other members' personal growth and success is extraordinary. It's not unusual for members of such teams to sacrifice individual rewards to secure success and rewards for the team. The degree of coordination and interdependency within the team is such that team members are able to anticipate what each other will need and provide it in advance.

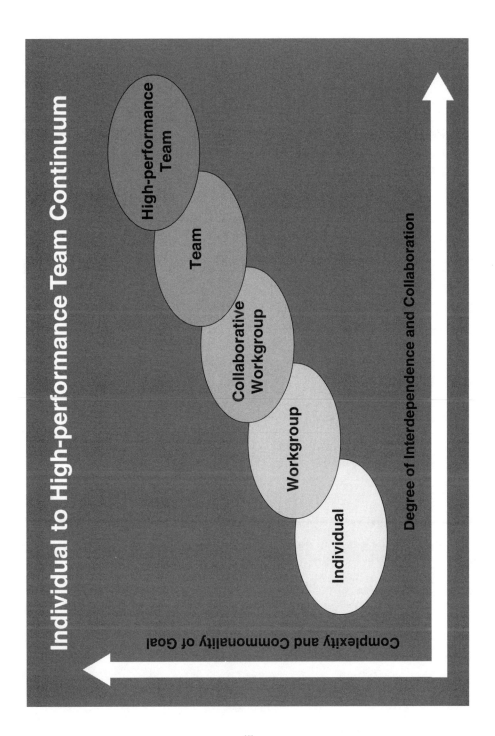

Individual to High-performance Team Continuum

High-performance Team

Team

Collaborative Workgroup

Workgroup

Individual

Degree of Interdependence and Collaboration

Complexity and Commonality of Goal

Suited for Work – Getting a Good Fit

Using the Individual to High-performance Team Continuum illustrated on page 15, complete this worksheet to determine what kind of work unit fits best with your assigned task. Note that the need for collaboration increases as the continuum moves from left to right, from individual to high-performing team. This movement reflects the greater need for collaboration as the work grows more complex.

Thoroughly describe the nature of the task to be completed.

Is the task simple and one-dimensional or is it complex and multidimensional?

What types of barriers and problems might have to be addressed and solved in order to successfully complete the task?

In order to complete the task, what types of decisions might have to be made? What boundaries or constraints might apply to these decisions?

Will the task be recurrent or will it only occur once?

How long will it take to complete the task?

How readily available are the information, knowledge, and skills required to complete the task?

Is a subject matter expert available who has all the information, knowledge, and skills required to complete the task?

Does the task require the efforts of several people who all have the same or similar expertise, knowledge, and skills?

How important is diversity of thought and opinion in the successful completion of the task?

How critical are relationships with key stakeholders, customers, internal clients, and top management to the successful completion of the task?

If You Need a Team, You Need Support

You may have decided at this point that achieving the results your organization is asking for clearly warrants forming a team. But no team works in a vacuum. Teams have to function in the context of your organization and its culture. Recruiting team members doesn't guarantee that they will work as a team. Even if you choose the individual members with great care and regard to their skills and expertise, the group may never jell into a team. If your organization can't or won't support the team you've decided to form, or if it won't reward team achievements the same way it recognizes individual achievements, then the success of your team will be diminished. You and your organization may be better off addressing critical business challenges by some other kind of work unit.

For example, if your organization won't give teams authority outside of the chain of command (although reporting to the organization), it isn't likely to get results from a team formed to explore solutions that cross functional boundaries. If your organization doesn't support the idea that a team should be comprised of skilled people with diverse viewpoints, then your team may have problems reaching consensus, making strategic decisions, or providing innovative perspectives on business challenges. If your organization doesn't have the time to allow a team to develop, then it may struggle to form an effective team (which takes longer to get results than does another kind of work unit).

To determine if your organization can support a team – if it really needs a team – check out its support systems. Organizational resources include traditional types of resources like budgets, the appropriate staff, and the necessary space and technology for team members, as well as development programs, team-oriented financial systems, and systems that provide public company-wide support.

Assessing Your Organization's Support for Teams

To understand the support your organization is likely to give a team, identify what kind of team-oriented resources and processes it has in place. Use the following questions to assess your organization's support of teams in the areas of development programs, financial systems, and mechanisms to show company-wide support.

Development Programs. In order for a team to be effective, organizations need to provide development programs that teach some of the basic interpersonal competencies and team processes necessary for teamwork.

- Does the organization offer any form of training for teams in such areas as conflict management, collaboration, and team-performance 360-degree surveys?

- If the organization does not have any formal training for teams, is it acceptable to go outside the organization for that training?

- Where does the training budget reside? Is it part of the team's budget? Is it part of the individual development budget? Is the money in a centralized organization budget?

- If there are no training dollars, is there a process for making comparative team visits (teams visit other teams in other organizations to learn)?

Financial Systems. Teams often cross over functional areas, but many organizations tie financial systems to single functional areas. Organizations need to provide financial systems that support teams and policies that ensure that team budgets are protected.

- How does the budget process work within the organization when creating a team?

- What are the budgetary implications if a team is made up of individuals from different functional areas that have their own independent budgets?

- What needs to be done to make sure that the team will have its own budget without any strings attached?

- If the team needs additional money, what is the process for getting that money?

Public and Company-wide Support. It takes more than a sponsor and an e-mail announcement to support a team. Organizations should provide effective and consistent communication tools and channels that support the team and appropriate political support to gain company-wide endorsement for the team's work.

- Are there examples within your organization of successful teams? What processes were put in place to make that team successful? How was support for those successful teams communicated, not only at the top, but throughout the organization?

- Who within your organization has successfully led a team? What could you learn from them?

- For the teams that were not effective, what contributed to their not being successful from the organization's perspective?

Team Rewards. Beyond the three support areas just described, organizations also support teams through reward systems that recognize group achievement alongside or even in place of individual achievements. If your organization doesn't sponsor such rewards, then it doesn't need to sponsor teams. To assess your organization's team reward support, consider the following questions:

- How does your organization reward team performance?
- What examples have you seen of special efforts to show appreciation for especially effective team performance?
- How does the organization balance rewards between individual efforts and team accomplishments?
- What tangible, nonmonetary rewards are typically provided to teams in your organization?

Go Team

Given the necessary support and resources, and the right mandate, teams provide exceptional value to organizations. In a complex world and in complex organizations, very little can be accomplished by a single individual. Business challenges often need the diversity of ideas and the close collaboration that characterize teams.

When employees work and experience success as team members, they often find the work to be particularly satisfying. The larger perspective that teams can provide to individual members often allows them to find greater meaning in their work. Teams often become a key feature to an organization's being perceived as

Working on Teams Benefits Individuals

Serving as a team member is a key developmental experience. Team membership gives employees:

- a chance to get out of their "silos" and "my job" mentality

- a new network of contacts in the organization that can facilitate and speed future projects and routine business processes

- opportunities to leverage individual knowledge and skills

- a means to understanding the needs and functions of many parts of the organization

- opportunities to formulate and articulate ideas and present opinions

- opportunities to develop leadership abilities

- the experience of collaboration in solving problems and in making a difference.

a good place to work, fostering the employee commitment and loyalty that all organizations want.

Your organization may need teams for its own good. Teams are often the best means by which organizations can learn. They are innovation engines and are often the best chance for building new ideas, products, services, and solutions. But teams are not the best answer for every business challenge. They may not even be a good answer. To get the powerful benefits that teams promise, managers need to be sure that a team is what is needed for any specific business goal, and that the organization will support a team in its work.

Suggested Readings

Dyer W. G. (1995). *Team building, current issues and new alternatives* (3rd ed.). Reading, MA: Addison-Wesley.

Hughes, R. L., Ginnett, R. C., & Curphy, G. J. (1996). *Leadership: Enhancing the lessons of experience* (2nd ed.). Boston, MA: Irwin McGraw-Hill.

Katzenbach, J. R. (1998). *Teams at the top: Unleashing the potential of both teams and individual leaders.* Boston, MA: Harvard Business School Press.

Katzenbach, J. R., & Smith, D. K. (1993). *The wisdom of teams.* Boston, MA: Harvard Business School Press.

Nadler, D. A. (1998). Executive team effectiveness: Teamwork at the top. In D. A. Nadler, J. L. Spencer, & Associates (Eds.), *Executive teams.* San Francisco: Jossey-Bass.

Scholtes, P. R., Joiner, B. L., & Streibel, B. J. (1996). *The team handbook* (2nd rev. ed.). Madison, WI: Oriel Inc.

Sessa, V. I., Hansen, M. C., Prestridge, S., & Kossler, M. E. (1999). *Geographically dispersed teams: An annotated bibliography.* Greensboro, NC: Center for Creative Leadership.

Background

Since the mid 1980s, the Center for Creative Leadership (CCL) has developed team-building initiatives for scores of companies across a wide range of industries. During this time CCL has interviewed team members, team leaders, team sponsors, and other employees within those companies to gather information on team performance, team leadership, team support, and team results. Because of that information, which CCL continues to gather and analyze, CCL is able to present customized materials and initiatives to organizations seeking to improve the effectiveness of their teams.

In 1990 that knowledge and experience was embedded into two of CCL's educational initiatives: Leadership and Teamwork (LAT), and Leadership and High-Performance Teams (LHPT). In 2000 LAT was folded into the LHPT program, which continues to provide a hands-on experience for team leaders that emphasizes a range of practical tools and strategies for enhancing the performance of any team. The program provides research-based information about how high-performance teams work; honest appraisals of existing teams' strengths and weaknesses; and proven approaches for turning average performers into a highly effective team. It covers such issues as selecting team members, launching teams effectively, bridging cross-cultural differences in teams, and resolving team conflict.

In addition to these educational programs, CCL launched in 1996 a research project into the work and performance of geographically dispersed teams. Since 1997, various CCL faculty members have presented their findings and analyses at conferences and through various publications. That research helps to further inform CCL's classroom content.

CCL continues its work with clients and with other scholars to further develop its understanding of teams – how they can be led more effectively, how they can best achieve organizational goals, and how they can be created and maintained for improved results. Through educational programs like LHPT, CCL seeks to pass that understanding on to team leaders and their organizations in order that teams meet and even surpass performance expectations.

Key Point Summary

Teams can address many business challenges, replacing individual effort with group strength. They enable some companies to take giant leaps forward, becoming faster, more innovative, and more responsive to markets and customers.

But teams are not always the best way to meet a business challenge. Teams are expensive and time consuming to launch, and leading a team is a full-time job. Before you launch a team to meet the tasks your organization has placed before you, consider whether or not you need a team to get results.

Teams are a good choice for addressing complex problems and issues that affect many parts of the organization and its people. But for decisions that must be reached quickly, or when a diversity of perspectives is not needed, smaller and more easily managed work units are a better choice. Before launching a team, analyze the task at hand to make sure that a team is the kind of work unit best fit to address the challenge.

Work units that traditionally exist in organizations include individuals, workgroups, collaborative workgroups, teams, and high-performance teams. The situations best suited for each of these work units depends on the complexity of the challenge and the degree of collaboration needed to meet that challenge.

Before you can decide whether or not you need a team you will also need to determine if your organization is going to support a team. Without organizational support, your team cannot easily achieve its objectives. If your organization can't back a team with development programs, financial systems, mechanisms to show company-wide support, and rewards, then it shouldn't form a team (which will likely perform poorly or fail to meet objectives).

Teams are innovation engines and often the best chance for building new ideas, products, services, and solutions. To get the powerful benefits that teams promise, managers need to be sure that a team is what is needed for any specific business goal, and that the organization will support a team in its work.

Order Form

To order, complete and return a copy of this form or contact the Center's Publication Area at: Post Office Box 26300 • Greensboro, NC 27438-6300 • Phone 336-545-2810 • Fax 336-282-3284. You can also order via the Center's online bookstore at www.ccl.org/publications

	QUANTITY	SUBTOTAL
❏ I would like to order additional copies of **Do You Really Need a Team?** (#412) $8.95 ea.*		
❏ I would like to order other Ideas Into Action Guidebooks.		
❏ **Ongoing Feedback** (#400) $8.95 ea.*		
❏ **Reaching Your Development Goals** (#401) $8.95 ea.*		
❏ **Becoming a More Versatile Learner** (#402) $8.95 ea.*		
❏ **Giving Feedback to Subordinates** (#403) $8.95 ea.*		
❏ **Three Keys to Development** (#404) $8.95 ea.*		
❏ **Feedback That Works** (#405) $8.95 ea.*		
❏ **Communicating Across Cultures** (#406) $8.95 ea.*		
❏ **Learning from Life** (#407) $8.95 ea.*		
❏ **Keeping Your Career on Track** (#408) $8.95 ea.*		
❏ **Preparing for Development** (#409) $8.95 ea.*		
❏ **Choosing an Executive Coach** (#410) $8.95 ea.*		
❏ **Setting Your Development Goals** (#411) $8.95 ea.*		
❏ **Feedback Package** (#724; includes #400, #403, #405) $17.95 ea.		
Add sales tax if resident of CA (7.5%), CO (6%), NC (6%)	**SALES TAX**	
U.S. shipping (UPS Ground – $4 for 1st book; $0.95 each additional book) Non-U.S. shipping (Express International – $20 for 1st book; $5 each additional book)	**SHIPPING**	
CCL's Federal Tax ID #23-707-9591	**TOTAL**	

*Single title quantity discounts: 5-99 – $7.95; 100-499 – $6.50; 500+ – $5.95

DISCOUNTS ARE AVAILABLE
IF ORDERING BY MAIL OR FAX, PLEASE COMPLETE INFORMATION BELOW.

PAYMENT

❏ My check or money order is enclosed. **(Prepayment required for orders less than $100.)**

❏ Charge my order, plus shipping, to my credit card.
    ❏ American Express   ❏ Discover   ❏ MasterCard   ❏ Visa

Acct. # _____   Expiration Date: Mo./Yr. _____

Signature _____

SHIP TO

Name _____

Title _____

Organization _____

Street Address _____

City/State/Zip _____

Phone (   ) _____
Your telephone number is required for shipping.

❏ **CHECK HERE TO RECEIVE A COMPLETE GUIDE TO CCL PUBLICATIONS.**
❏ **CHECK HERE TO RECEIVE INFORMATION ABOUT CCL PROGRAMS AND PRODUCTS.**

ORDER BY PHONE: 336-545-2810 • ONLINE: WWW.CCL.ORG/PUBLICATIONS